Dining on Words

By Lisbeth L. McCarty

Explanation of Title

When I go to a restaurant and really love the food I am served, I will return to that restaurant numerous times. For me, poetry is like dining in that sense. I love to return again and again to the words I love so much.

I have returned many times to read "The Raven" by Edgar Allen Poe. I am once again mystified by the talking bird that perches above his door and delighted with all the rhymes involved in the poem. Who else would have ever thought to rhyme 'lent thee' with 'nepenthe' in such a magnificent manner?

I also love to return to the poetry of Robert Frost, especially "Stopping by Woods on a Snowy Evening." He gives such a beautiful interpretation of falling snow in a forest. Reading this poem causes my soul to soar with delight.

I have an appreciation for the masterful choice of words in the poem "Harlem" by the poet Langston Hughes. He asks whether a dream deferred would dry up "line a raisin in the sun." This line was so perfect that it resulted in Lorraine Hansberry using the line to name her play "A Raisin in the Sun."

Thus, I was compelled to design this book of poetry like a dining experience, starting with an amuse bouche represented by a short, playful poem. Next, the haikus without titles form the variety of appetizers being set before you. The soup and salad course represents both rhymed and unrhymed poetry. The main entrée is a mixture of a proteins and vegetables represented by enigmatic thoughts. Finally, the last course is dessert, once again a haiku, which represents happy times of celebration. Please enjoy dining on the supper of words I have created for you.

Amuse Bouche

Clumsy Couplets

My feet take me where I want to go
Until I fall, then it isn't so.

I tripped over a piece of dirt
And fell right through the earth

No time to sound alarms
You saved me in your arms

I am forever indebted
A fact I've never regretted

Our to-the-altar route
Started with this meet-cute

Where's My Dinner?

Ordering food for delivery can be oh, so great
Until they don't get the order straight
There are so many things that can go so wrong
Half the items on my order were gone

I called the restaurant, but they passed the blame
Said the delivery service was rather lame
I called that service, but I was stunned
When they only offered a $5 refund

"The missing items cost more than a fin,"
I said, sure I was reflecting chagrin
After haggling, the refund was finally fair
For lack of a full meal, this was all I could bear

Now, I always go to the restaurant in person
So my dining experience will not worsen
The lesson I learned that gave me a fright
Is that no longer is the customer always right

APPETIZERS

The rain stopped falling
Outside, sparrows sing loudly
Breathing the ions

Love you much, mean it
Terse does not negate the truth
Do you believe me?

Ear on ground hears hum
The ferocious sun warms earth
In yellow meadow

Six across stumps me
Seven letters for scary
Aha! Phobia

The child ties her shoes
Left foot, right foot are reversed
Still, accomplishment

Ovals dot her “i”s
Strange choice of penmanship
For an attorney

His almond-shaped eyes
Stare deep into my cold soul
And warm my sad heart

Mandelbot's fractals
Changed the outlook of the world
Already in place

Wide complexity
Rooted in simplicity
Shows in ice crystals

SOUP AND SALAD COURSE

Wind

Wind
All over
But never seen

Wind
Whistling
Heard by all

Wind
Gentle or wild
Hold your hat

Is it True?

I didn't even get to say goodbye
They are gone
Never underestimate
An incapacitated guardian
Or a determined enemy
Always check their lungs
For any kind of evidence

Unforeseen Circumstances

No one had time to intervene
The explosion was without composure
We almost lost all hope
We soldiered on
To save the children
To save Christmas
We will refuse to be obtuse
We will let our demons loose
And we will not
Be robbed of precious lives

MAIN COURSE

The Autumn of Contentment

The leaves display a panoply of a rainbow's colors
These are tree discards as Nature's attainable experience in pleasant hues
From the wide-branched tress, the leaves drop slowly and silently
Down into scratchy patches of dirt amid brown, expiring grass
The leaves add boldness by the very trait of their decay,
Poking their colorful, vein-lined faces through the familiar annual wreckage
Like shells that children of summer have stuffed into a bucket of sand from the beach
But the leaves have more reds, oranges yellows, greens, and purples dotting the landscape
And unlike a summer day, the sun barely warms the atmosphere
Instead, the chill in the air is a whispering harbinger of the gray, harsh winter to come soon
And cover the ground with a blanket of glaring, white, blinding snow
Yet, think not about the coldness ahead
Instead, breathe in the glorious cornucopia of autumn
Watch Saturdays' children in sweaters and light jackets
Jump into piles of leaves
Shrieking with delight and giggling with the silliness of pure play
In such abandonment, there's a hope and a future
To give us strength to forge through past the end of the year
In this sense, feel safe to know
That autumn is the new spring

Face v. Face

I used to stand before the mirror
Darken my lashes with mascara
Blush my cheeks with rouge
Redden my lips with liner

I would fluff my hair
One last time
Then, give myself a mental okay
To go face the world

I do not like mirrors now
They are traitors
Lying to me when I look in them
My face is gone

The mirror shows a creviced face, droopy eyelids
Permanently turned-down corners of the mouth
Thinning gray hair on the head
Eyebrows that stopped growing at the midway mark

Where did my looks go?
Where did my time go?
Where did my memory go?
I curse the stupid mirror

The Speed of Change

When you opened your eyes
I was hypnotized
A friend that goes the length
Gives me so much strength

Something went terribly wrong
A dirge became our song
There arose so much strife
Can I justify my life?

Non-existent Scenario

The red flags set off flames
I have myself to blame
I clearly ignored the signs
I quickly shut down my mind

For a time, it was stupendous
But you were never generous
And all the crazy folly
Just led to melancholy

I don’t understand the relationship
Playing out on a projected filmstrip
I now have learned to bury
A boyfriend who is imaginary

Holiday Bouquet

The aroma of relatives is in the air
Just like every Christmas
Aunt Margaret still uses her bottle of drug-store perfume
She received as a gift in 1971 from her daughter Brooklyn
Margate uses this gift so sparingly through the years
That the scent has turned from pleasant to cloying
Mom's hands are thick with the smell of turkey
That she rose to baste every hour
Throughout the night and morning
Dad has the smell of fresh blood emanating from his shin
Caused by his annual run-in with the coffee table,
The table that is moved to an awkward place each December
To make room for the pine tree
With its wonderful scent of freshness
Among the glittering tinsel and glowing string lights
The dog, Sparrow, oozes the unmistakable odor
That is a mixture of wet nose and thick, matted fur
Plus canine shame for the present he tore into under the tree
A gift which was not Sparrows to open
My cousin Jenna has scents of pine cones and cinnamon
Dabbed behind her dangling snowman earrings
Her boyfriend Jeb reeks of cigarettes and late-night bars
Of Dirty feet and busted teeth
And an entire future of bad decisions and corrupted morals
The holiday displays a cornucopia of life in fragrances
Good and bad and everything in between
Brooklyn, the oldest grandchild, reminds Nana
To remember the reception sticks

DESSERT

Fluffy birthday cake
Smashed by a child's tiny hands
Toddlers do not care

-The End-

www.ingramcontent.com/pod-product-compliance
Lightning Source LLC
LaVergne TN
LVHW080600160826
845677LV00010B/1935
* 9 7 9 8 9 8 6 3 2 1 5 9 2 *